"Using in-jokes, old arguments and absurdities, Kent Johnson satirizes the 'ruthless kid-poets with their little cymbals and bells.' Yet satire's bleak irreverence is also a kind of intimacy: we can't mock what we don't know well. More earnestly, *Nuper Verba* urges us to 'make lasting song of our loss, /That it may rise above the shallow attentions of our clan.' Pay attention, then, to these poems. Say poetry is a haunted mansion or a freakish funhouse. There, a hall of mirrors ceases to reflect the tiresome egoism of poetry culture and instead offers 'endless selves receding, tinier and tinier, until' one can no longer see oneself. We knew we were there, far back, but we were also gone. That, Johnson shows us, is where poetry truly has the last word."

—Elizabeth Robinson

"Kent Johnson is notorious for his mordant wit and tenacious satire, turned, more often than not, on the contemporary poetry scene. In the past, his ironic stance has been a massive, defensive engine against the crass, the venal, the insufferably narcissistic. Now, in *Nuper Verba*, wit and satire are subsumed, having become a given, and a new horizon opens before us. What Yeats, translating Swift's epitaph, calls 'savage indignation' is still there, but, especially in the magnificent Horatian Odes, a passionate honesty and vulnerability emerge to complement the intelligence of Johnson's provocations. There has been nothing like them since Pound's 'Homage to Sextus Propertius'. This is a gorgeous, heartbreaking book."

—Norman Finkelstein

"As a poet, I do and do not know why anyone would take up the vocation today, especially when just being human is considered by many to be despicable in itself. But I don't know. When I read Kent's work, I want to believe in the authority of poetry again. I know that it still exists, right here, with me and others, outside of the bullshit, outside of the Poetry Foundation, out of reach of all those so-called poet laureates out there, outside of the institutions vying for power, outside of the popular poets dying for even more attention, leaving their cheap verses all over the internet like trending memes. The thought that poetry might not exist without all of these contentions and contradictions, though, really troubles my sleep. But then this makes me think I know what it is that Kent's work does; it acknowledges a mystery. Maybe the only mystery: that Poetry could be writing all of us into existence, orchestrating this whole realm with authority built on ephemerality and balance, like some invisible but compassionate network of Chaos. Again, I don't know. Read *Nuper Verba* because you don't really have a choice."

—Carlos Lara

"In the central sequence of *Nuper Verba*, fifteen 'Horatian Odes,' satirist, analyst, and sometimes starter of poetry wars Kent Johnson returns to one of the origins of Western lyric in lines by turn barbed, laugh-out-loud, and delicately touching. Transformed ('transcreated' or 'translucinated' in Johnson's own terms) from their Latin originals and prior English translations, these poems often express 'in my last days' the opposite of the satirist's desire: 'I want to be dulcis and not acidus, believe me.' For all their self-reflexive layering, their comic allusiveness, their unremitting takedowns of poetic careerism meeting Horace's own self-ironizing aspirations to poetic immortality, these are also autobiographical poems about Johnson's own life, career, and political and intellectual commitments. Tutelary spirits like Edward Dorn—perhaps the chemo-ridden satirist of *Chemo Sabe*—appear in Johnson's ode to satyr-ists, as irony and energetic vitriol is clamped and silenced in the Scold's Bridle: 'stammer, satire, your pitiful last...' And yet the familiar impulse remains: 'Yes, tell me I am among the / Poets'—that itch, somewhere between impulse and deep conviction against all the odds, that runs from Horace to the Williams of 'The Desert Music' to 'Kentuvius Maximus in his / Big house.' Here 'my heart belongs to ... a torn, Janus-faced god' both of scorching satire and lyric poignancy, of public vituperation and private loss in 'this arbor's darkening shade'."

—Alan Golding

"Detained in his wound, everything becomes observable. The aching cave forever open. He blesses us in the evenings and frightens us in the mornings. No bridges to burn. He is the warning that is spoken of."

—MTC Cronin

Kent Johnson

Nuper Verba

Horatian Odes
Tavern Jokes
Spectral Tales

Shearsman Books

First published in the United Kingdom in 2022 by
Shearsman Books Ltd
PO Box 4239
Swindon
SN3 9FN

Shearsman Books Ltd Registered Office
30–31 St. James Place, Mangotsfield, Bristol BS16 9JB
(this address not for correspondence)

www.shearsman.com

ISBN 978-1-84861-857-2

ACKNOWLEDGMENTS
Some poems from the section titled 'Horatian Odes' were published in the
chapbook *After Horace*, from Longhouse Publishers. Other poems from that
section were featured by Jerome Rothenberg at his *Poetry & Poetics* blog, as well
as at *Jacket2* magazine. While most of the Tavern Jokes are my inventions, some
are adapted from folk versions of "a guy walks into a bar" classics. The section
'The Clouds, The Birds, The Frogs' was published in a limited-edition
chapbook from If a Leaf Falls Press. My sincere thanks to the editors
who first published parts of this collection.

Contents

Foreword

The thing I love most about Kent Johnson's work is how it always puts me back on my heels. You just never know what this guy is going to throw at you. Horatian Odes? Poetry Bar Jokes? Spectral Tales? Kent Johnson is dedicated to poetry as the *Open* of language, or, say, to language opening through poetry. Hence the perpetual surprise. It is a suspension of habit, or maybe the transformation and deformation of habit, the radical conservation of habit in uninhibited imaginations of further. It is a master note of Johnson's entire body of work, the heart of his struggle to hang on and let go at the same time.

Take his perennial interest in poetry's past, the forms earlier poets invented for their own purposes that many contemporary poets dismiss as antique. Even as a form, say a Horatian Ode, embodies a residue of a particular moment, it continues to offer possibilities of further opening to those open to it, those who understand poetry's continual potential for rehabilitation, which is to say how to re-inhabit it. I don't think I have met anyone who knows as much about poetry as Kent Johnson, where *knows* is not just some academic mastery of details, but a somatic passion, a cellular intensity.

You'd never know it looking at him. Looking at Kent Johnson, if you looked at him at all, you'd think, there goes an ordinary guy. And if you sat down at his table in some hole-in-wall bar in the mountains of Idaho where he and the grizzled guy at the next table were comparing notes on the rainbows and cutthroat trout they had landed (and released) that day, that's what you'd think, too. Till he turns around, smiles and says hi, and starts saying the most interesting things about Jack Spicer or Horace or César Vallejo or Ovid or H.D. or some ancient Chinese poets you never even heard of. His range of reading is immense and multilingual. Growing up in Uruguay helped. He is a natural born trans-nationalist and that trans-nationalist knowledge/orientation led him to immerse himself in the work of poets Eastern, Western, ancient, modern and in between. The thing is, he just loves poetry, really loves it, all of it. He lives and breathes it. And not as a "profession" or "career." More like a woman wailing for her demon lover.

The surprises in this book come at you thick and furious. Often, it's through the simple-seeming but deceptively complex and sophisticated *this-and-that* mode he picked up from the early New York scene and brought to his reading of Horace who, it turns out, could have been a

New York poet. With Johnson, though, you never end up where you think you're headed. His wild and un-cinctured imagination inevitably takes you through twists and turns that leave you breathless even as his tonal range seamlessly moves from laughter to despair, from elegy to joy, from grief over his own looming mortality to laughter at the absurdity of our condition.

Then there's his thing about inventing and/or playing around with genres. Especially obscure genres like his *faits divers*, or in this case, poetry bar jokes. Everybody knows bar jokes, but not bar jokes quite like these. This is not only the first book of poetry to include poetry bar jokes so far as I know but also the only one. And that's because Kent invented the genre. But that's true of so much of Johnson's work, including his *epigrammititis*, his metered doggerel, and his murky association with contemporary Fluxus-like events such as the Yasusada affair, or the O'Hara/Koch authorship scandal. Invention and reinvention are integral to his sense of poetry's calling, which is to speak truth in all its facets.

And likely as not, his invention will be driven by his fierce love of poetry and his moral defense of its integrity in the face of the corrupting energies of the post-New American Poetry neo-liberal counter-revolution which has been set on dragging poetry back into sanctioned institutional locales after its brief escape from them in the 1960s. In that regard, Kent Johnson is one of the only contemporary masters of satire (André Spears is the other one), a once popular genre of poetry now fallen on hard times. Satire just isn't fashionable in an academic poetry world. The essence of satire is the thinking of truth, of *telling it like it is*, as we once used to say. It means bringing to light the reality masked by various duplicities and hypocrisies, the unacknowledged contradictions between words and actions.

Not many poets today have the guts for that engagement. Assuming there is a "truth" at all is enough to get you ridiculed in certain learned quarters. And gods help you if you trigger someone, which is quite likely, given that lots of people really don't like that light illuminating their own indiscretions and dishonesties. Also, and this is kind of weird, in the 70s the whole poetry industry got infected with a virus called *sincerity* that is inimical to satire's creative duplicity. Whether it was the *your-true-voice-sincere* of creative writing endeavor or the *rested-totality-sincere* of Zukofsky's objectivism, it manifested in a rejection of, even an animosity toward, *the play of identity*, identity as a token, a rhetorical tool in pursuit of the revelation of difficult truths. Sincerity, whatever the original impulse, became identified with something like *authenticity*, a problematical category in poetry, if there ever was one. Satire looks upon such a situation with great relish.

It's safe to say that no other poet in North America today writes like Kent Johnson. He is a oner, and *Nuper Verba* is a Kent Johnson *tour de force*. It will leave you stunned, laughing, crying, enraged, enlightened, thoughtful, but above all else, astonished. You have been warned.

—Michael Boughn
Toronto, August 2022

Debi, Brooks, and Aaron… My love always.

HORATIAN ODES

Liber I, Ode 1

Maecenas, my shield and mask, scion of Poet Laureates,
Good friend, loather of prizes and grants—the variegated scraps
In this field give variegated people much pleasure. Lots of them feel it
Mainly on their vitae: tires screeching on the Olympic oval, polished
Sedans banking around the turn to cross the line and win the
Wreath—Glory in the Academy of Imperial Poets that makes them feel
Anointed by the jism of gods. Many covet approval from their fussy
Peeps; and others, the knowledge that troublesome Libyan troubadours
have been restored to their rank of yore. Verily, we know that if we treat
The heart properly it never gets tired. But if we run very hard, or swim
Very hard, or do anything of that kind, we suddenly throw a great
Deal of extra work upon the heart. For example, the self-publishing
Poet loves to peck around her small pile of dirt, and no amount of NEA
Cash could give her sea legs for the Real Ocean. And those waters
Panic the MFA holder, who starts to weep for his institutional womb
During a little storm, though as soon as it's good weather he's busy
Swabbing his deck for some new voyage, clueless he will
Fall over the edge of the earth. Many love drugs and booze
And always find some idle time to drink or shoot up by an idyllic stream.
Many people crave the thrill of Poetry War, also, rushing to the bugle call
Their Officers have commanded. Therefore, the deer cries forlornly
In its snare, trembling as if delicately held by a thread of quartz; when
The Poetry Warriors turn toward the bugle's sound, they do not see that
When a ray of light plays on the caught creature, it becomes dark and
Still, as if brushed by Diana's hand.

It's a spray of ivy, that Laurel of Poets, that I require to believe I consort
With the gods way up there. It's the lyric prance of nymphs and satyrs
That I cherish—Fashioned by the nine muses far back in a lost wood,
Secreted from the common crowd, the wood where Euterpe teases her
Flute, and Polyhymnia strokes the lyre: Yes, tell me I am among the
Poets and I will contrive that I am a god—knocking against the stars
With the crown of my acclaimed head.

Liber I, Ode 11

Don't fret, dear, we're hardly privy to
The fateful day the gods have assigned us.
Here's my suggestion: Ignore the Zodiac
Of the Po-Biz Astro Poets. Best to just

Accept what's allotted us, be it ninety-some
Winters, until we're embalmed and rigid, or
One last season, this one, where we fall in the
Snow, out for a stroll, like Robert Walser.

How could we explain to them his gentle prayer,
That nature, not art, might usurp the canvas?
He chose his solitary despair for a snowdrop subject,
Making it vast, like ruined buildings.

That's a poach from Ashbery, pretty much… Filter some
Wine, cut down on selfies, decant whatever you have
Into something more selfless, like Dickinson, or Oppen,
Say. Stop obsessing over the years left, like some poem in

The New Yorker. Think more of this moment, for there won't
Be another of its form. Fleeting Time is covetous, as I write this, even
Whilst the smallest particles of you demur, infinite and baffling.
Whether morning or night, the world's light cannot be grasped.

Liber I, Ode 16

So, about my satires: Entomb them, immolate them,
I don't care, toss the whole ash heap in the Dead
Sea-- do it, now, before the critics get them, heed
Me, fairest mother of fairest days.

You know what used to most make me want to grind corn
With my butt? Not Dindymene, the Department Chair,
Nor the Dean, who lives with the Big Snake, nor the
Ruthless kid-poets with their little cymbals and bells. No…

It was my chronic dander. Noric axes cannot dismember it,
The ship-sucking sea cannot drown it, whirlwinds
Cannot scatter it, the gods themselves cannot tame it.
Here they come, roaring down, all perfumed and dazzling.

Prometheus did his best at the creation: He sprinkled a bit
Of dust from gentle seals and tanagers into our raw clay,
But he couldn't resist a bit of powder, the rascal, from
The hearts of lions, driven mad by four-pawed gout.

Thus, the bile that broke Thyestes into four, on its
Rack, scores of glorious cities on mountains and plains
Got wrecked by it, from without and from within. Now
Farmers plough where the dead of ages enrich the earth.

Try to let it go. Do yoga, or something. Take a walk. And
Yet, and yet… after I do, I still feel that old pull. A cauldron
Burned in me when I was young and not ill. And even now,
In my last days, I cannot fully shake the mad lion's gout.

I want to be dulcis and not acidus, believe me, fairest mother.
I want all poets to be my friends, but they won't have me.
I want to give them back my broken heart. But my heart belongs
To the god who made it. And he is a torn, Janus-faced god.

Liber I, Ode 24

A great poet has departed. How might we grieve? Muse of
Sorrows, reveal to us our proper demeanor, transcending the
common, transient laments. Help us make lasting song of our loss,
That it may rise above the shallow attentions of our clan.

The caked cinnabar and kohl adorned his dead face. Plebeians and
Patricians clogged the aqueducts and streets. Augustus spoke
With emotion to the man's eminence, while Official Poets on the
Rostrum nodded solemnly as the virtues were extolled.

The ashes of Quintilius are now scattered by the wind. Such grandeur
And constancy will never be matched; such integrity and propriety
Are models beyond our grasp. Cliff cascades drum the silence of a
Thousand mountains. Who can manage such distances of the heart?

In a fortnight, everything will be OK. Poets will be petting each
Other's back, and petitions for honors will be flying like autumn
Leaves. Dark gossip will be whispered behind the arras. You weep
For no purpose, Virgil: He is gone and won't be back to redeem us.

Liber I, Ode 38

No prizes from trickster Eris for me, young poet,
Nor grants secretly filamented to oil or imperial wars.
I forbid you to scrounge-up, for sake of my vanity, any
Late-bloom garland of salvia and goldenrod.

Wood nettle now suits me for a crown just fine, grazie. And
Yes, far from the Rappahannock, the silent Arno moves along
Toward the sea. I can't get that sweet verse out of my blistering
Head, as I sip my sour linctus, in this arbor's darkening shade.

Liber I, Ode 39

Errant and ominous things, now. Hannibal courts the Seleucids.
As ever, exaltations in the Senate for the rule of global Republican markets.

The sub-rosa gatherings now with the panicked Greeks. Plus, the
desperation of Philip the Macedonian—the traitor—a minor dramatist, besides.

But this is what it's come to: Consul Fulvius Nobilior betrays chronic fidgets
and rashes. Consul Manlius Vulso exhibits boils and symptoms of paranoia.

Ah, the advisors in the intelligence agencies don't look as sapient as the editors of
the *Acta Diurna*—the obscenely obsequious *Acta Diurna*—had made them out to be.

The situation—whispers clueless Acilius Glabrio, the opposition's Speaker
in the Senate—is, like, really fucked up.

And even though we voted for War because we thought certain ancient
holy sites hid weapons of massive destruction,

Some kind of disposition must now be made (with an expected measure of hubris befitting Imperium) to appease the Seleucids.

Some peace delegations of supernatural disposition; an official State tour to holy sites of the vanquished heathens; a betrayed frisson for the gods of the mystic Orient…

Brave Scipio Africanus tells them to shove dildos up their timid bottoms. The glorious Battle of Magnesia is soon a rout. Now Philip is a piss-pot, and the Greeks our lapdogs.

Even as the white dust settles, Scipio Africanus makes a triumphal appearance at the Poetry Contest of Magnesia, where at the top of his lungs and with a colloquial twang

He praises the helmeted contenders and recites Lucilius and Terence. While the troops wildly acclaim the concurrence of his metrical savvy and plebeian authenticity…

Liber II, Ode 11

Ah, Quinctius, don't sweat it so much.
The Poetry Institutions or the Intel Agencies,
Whatever, can't touch us here. Sabine's an
Autonomous Zone. Their schemes are rubbish.

Vita brevis, my young friend. Soon youth and
Its illusions end. The teeth fall out, things go flaccid,
Insomnia rules. It's not all bad. In poetry, your tastes
Start to slide to the Greek and Chinese classics.

Don't fret the question of the infinite with your
Finitude. The world is full of mysteries and of
Wonders, and there's no need for us to puzzle
Ourselves by making any that do not really exist.

We are already in the Infinite, Quinctius. Let's drink
And smoke some hash under these trees while we're
Here, with these roses all around us and our bodies
Fragrant with balsam and myrrh from distant lands.

The gods of pleasure defeat the ghosts of worry.
Put aside your anger at the enemies of poetry for now.
You can write about them anon. Let's temper our cups of
Falernian fire with coldest water from this roaring stream.

Liber II, Ode 12

Who cares about dumb wars betwixt poets, Maecenas, bickering
Like mythological divinities? No one except poets, it seems! Prose
Suits that stuff much better than odes like mine: conceived by me in
Garland of musical phrase and not in sequence of a metronome.

Granted, the other day, when asked by Tacitus if the crucifixion of
6000 rebels along the Appian Way sixty years back by Crassus was
A "good idea," your bête noir Augustus solemnly said, "It is too
Early to tell." Tacitus guffawed. The Emperor glared.

Think about it, my dear: Fraught topics suit your temperament,
Such as quartering tyrants in the forum, or the latest bowel
Mishap of the editor who's rejected you. But why not try
My style, singing of sex, as I do about my squeeze, Licymnia?

She's my hottest Muse, not that she's the only one, female or not.
I've got groupies galore, ever since I won the Pulitzer and got invited
To read and dine at the Palatine… They each hope their heart will
Belong to only me. Their eyes gaze at me, shimmering with wine.

But who wants to snuggle-up with a glum satirist? Juvenal crows a lot,
But it's mainly for strut. His pecker's the size of my thumb. Trust me,
I know. And another thing: Who's going to end up in the Norton? Him,
Lucilius, Catullus, Martial, Persius? No, it will be me, dear benefactor!

Not that I couldn't unleash merciless fire, were it my death-bed desire.
Don't think Menippean spirit is all I've got in my quiver. This Horace is
No slouch and he proved it in his youth. So what if I'm now Official and
Have to watch my tongue a tad? In a flash, friend, I can fast rejoin you.

Liber II, Ode 15

Given the episteme, scythed lawns of latifundia will
Soon carpet fields where rough farms thrived in Cato's day.
Now bream ponds are bigger than fjords. Gauls drown in
Mock naval battles at galas MC'd by legionnaire bestsellers.

Plane trees will banish the august elms, with their canopied
Tunnels. Official versifiers go mad for wildflowers. Where once
Olives and millet ripened, the mawkish scent of Viola riviniana
Jams the big-house air. Poetry-groupies swoon and faint from it.

Strategically placed gazebos allow recovery under heavy laurels.
Sunstroke is leavened by stream-chilled wine during instruction
On glyconic and pherecratean meters. Romulus and Cincinnatus
Would spin in their graves. Not for them, the pompous plantations

Of these coddled grantees! They were more like communards,
Minding their little groves, their quail, and beehives, modest in
Means, not caring to erect some aqueduct-scale wall to trap the
Respite of its shade. If it was hot when you read Hipponax, well,

It was hot when you read Hipponax. Houses had roofs of straw
Back then, anyway, and no one gave it a second thought. But edicts
Obliged citizens to build bookcases out of good cedar and sacellums
From freshly cut marble. Citizens weren't gone in the belly or flabby

Of purpose. They reaped their own emmer and planted their
Own flora… joyous things, unburdened by anything but their
Beautiful natural blossoms and dew. Even as the dark blood
Dragged those bards down, too, with their enemies and their brothers.

Liber II, Ode 17

Why annoy me nonstop with your complaints, friend?
The gods will not have me fall before you yourself do,
Maecenas, sky-gable of my soul, redeemer and tributary
To my fans and benefactors in the Senate and at Palatine.

Should you be riven by lighting after one of my readings,
For instance, how could I, your lyrical ward, your double-self,
Make it? Fused as we are, we'll need to go in tandem. That
Would sure make the 6 PM news: Patron & Poet slain by Jupiter!

I made my solemn vow. When your day comes, so my own
Day it shall be. You and me, together, as one. I'm aware of my
Talent. But you are my conduit. And I don't have the stamina,
At this stage, to grovel for state grants or teaching positions.

Whether fair Libra, or choleric Scorpio, or luminous Capricorn
governed my birth, you and I are doubled stars. Jove saved
You from Saturn's eye, enfolding you in his fantastic wings,
Making the crowd stand and call you back for a triple encore.

In my lesser case, Faunus made that toppling pine swerve just so.
He, delegate of Mercury, protector of pirates and poets, compelled
Me to erect an adulterous altar, as sacrifice to the authentic hecatomb.
Let us be, now, both grateful and guilty. We shall offer up the lamb.

Liber II, Ode 19 [Abbreviatio]

Peeps, hear me out—It was great Dante himself. I saw him,
the very man, right there, fervent, by the eerie asphodels,
Chanting gentle Swift to Stella, to sweaty satyrs and nymphs.
Dante with goat feet!! Martial, Jonson, Pope, Parker, Koch,

Dorn, with goat feet! And their pointy ears? And their gum-hard
Hair pulled horizontalem, to such glossy point, three feet behind
Their ashen heads? My vision banged and clattered my unwell mind.
Yes, Helmet of Iron, my End. I did taunt them; now the Three Fates

Ironically taunt me. The Latin is nine stanzas longa. This breve traduction
But a timidus three. Quare? Because their Scold's Bridle bears a threesome
Of holes: Two for the eyes, one for the mouth, and pricked spike in
Tongue for lame, choliambic measure. Stammer, satire, your pitiful last...

Liber II, Ode 21
(Ambitious Hellenic Bards and Avaricious Roman Imitators)

Theocritus fancies the sullen Bollingen, tenebrous it goes.
Eubulus wants the deep and chary Pulitzer, umbral it flows.
Ibycus yearns for the turbid Pushcart, the color of brown stones.
Aeschylus is friending.

Herakleitos covets the turbulent Rense, effulgent it crashes and clangs.
Antimachus of Teos fancies the diffident Shahitya Akademi, its guttering light.
Nicander desea el MacArthur, poderosamente fluyendo.
Sappho is friending.

Euripedes has the jones for the frozen Newdigate, lambent it glows.
Hipponax aspires to the inscrutable Bobbitt, iridian and candescent.
Lasus desires the gray Gaisford, phlegmatic and demure.
Homer is unfriending.

Menander thirsts for the Aiken Taylor; blue and languorous it flows.
Menippus hungers for the Agha Shahid Ali; it slumbers across the bluish land.
Telecleides longs for the Lannan, its alluvia mounded and blue.
Aristophanes is trending.

Diagoras has a yen for the quiet Lilly, cretaceous and blanched.
Xenophon desires the Golden Wreath of Struga, shattered beneath the sun.
Philemon wishes for the Adonais, flaring beneath the sun.
Alcman is unfriending.

Callimachus desires the Val Vallis, gurgling caliginous in its moxie runs.
Aratus veut pour le Kim-Su-yông, pris dans la glace.
Cleophon covets the parlous Kavanagh, full of ominous, virescent stones.
Hesiod is friending.

Iophon has a thing for the Elder; fauna lapping its parched pools.
The gay Montreal overwhelms its quaint eyots; Philitas of Cos has eyes for it.
Eubulus covets the Alice James; a tributary of the Hawley, it rolls on.
Pindar is unfriending.

The Chelsea is lined with runes and ancient trash; Nikarchos dreams of it.
The broad Laughlin shores its ruins against the pylons; Eupolis desires it.
Elephantis is bent on the Castagnola; huge structures collapse to
                                                    saturnine foams.
Archilochus is friending.

Amphis wants the swollen Rattle, achronic and beclouded.
Chersias hankers after the Hardison, dredged and deep.
Evenus of Paros craves the icy Starrett, serpentine and blue.
Sextus Propertius on Esquiline Hill is a blackened stump.

Bion of Smyrna desires the Forward, pushing bravely along.
Melinno covets the Wallace Stevens, pushing against its leaden banks.
Herodas hungers for the Lenore Marshall, its banks carmine rose at dusk.
Ovid, exiled in Tomis, is poisoned by a wicked poet.

Sotades wishes for the stolid Frost, its banks nettled and dark.
Telesilla dreams of the gurgling Popescu, red embers along its banks.
Crinagoras of Myteline has the jones for the Kingsley Tufts, its osier-
                                                    clustered banks.
Gaius Valgius Rufus is evaporated in the Senate's garden.

Parrhasios wants the brooding Brittingham; indifferent it flows.
The Sandeen is clotted with ice; Ion of Chios has an itch for it.
Evenus of Paros désire le NBA, ses eaux implacables dévalant les pistes.
Bacchylides of Ceos is trending.

Choerilus of Iasos has eyes for the Vennum, its dependable velocities.
Choerilus of Samos wants the Isabella Gardner, obsidian as tar it goes.
Hermippus begehrt die starke und leise Nobel.
Marcus Manilius, imitator of Lucretius, is on fire.

Sositheus wishes for the Bridport, boats crashed against its stones.
Aristeas sueña con el Amy Lowell, susurrando sus secretos sin cesar.
Mesomedes has a yen for the Eliot, vatic amidst factories and debris.
Pindar is trending.

The concupiscent Braude breaks its chamois banks; Euphorion wants it.
The Alain-Grandbois is full of undertows; Nicarchus pines for it.
The Wilhelm Busch ist mit Logs gestaute; Panyassis es wünscht.
Sulpicia is chained by a crazed poet to a bed of thorns.

The Griffin roars its song in lateritious freshets; Quintus Smyrnaeus is
                                                              mad for it.
The Ballymaloe eats its loam banks in chunks; Dionysius Chalcus wants it.
The Neruda is red beneath the clanging sun; Rhyanus is hot for it.
Albius Tibullus, favorite of Marcus Valerius, is a blackened stump.

Iophon fancies the vestal Whitman, singing its flows through weird pools.
Nonnus of Patmos yearns for the plaintive Bynner, trailing its hoary
                                                       foam in snags.
The lonely Crab Orchard crashes against the dikes; Magnes yearns for it.
Grattius Faliscus, of sweet hexameters, has lost his family and his head.

Nossis desires the narrow Loewe, caliginous and bright it goes.
Agathon wants the solemn Cervantes, great oaks shading its quartz shoals.
Pherecrates wishes for the lightsome Jenko, though it is encased in ice.
Gaius Julius Hyginus has run into the forest chased by a witch.

Phileimon yearns for the Sarton; pale and hypnotic it rushes.
The Sawtooth is slow blue smoke; Asklepiades aches for it.
The banks of the Confrontation are aflame; Korinna fancies it.
Stesichoros of Metauros is friending.

The Frogmore breathes its poison mists; Aischylos has the jones for it.
The Pollak sucks and pools its wacked-out flows; Terpandros hankers for it.
Philodemos wants the riley Faber; it churns up houses and chariots in
                                                       flooded eddies.
I, Quintus Horatius Flaccus, am vaporized in the sun.

The Rabindra Puraskar does not dry in the terrible sun; Proklos craves it.
Kallinos desires the crazy Nobel; its turgid depths are full of crazy things.
Antipatros of Thessalonike wants the wild Vilenica; it washes
                                         huge metallic things out to sea.
Publius Vergilius Maro has been kidnapped by a pack of wolves.

The Shapcott blows up and kayaks go flying; Theognis thirsts for it.
The Leven is silent and etiolated, like bread; Didymos dreams of it.
Mnasalkas hungers for the Lampman; light streaks through it like hair.
Lucillius is trending.

Virgil craves the Griffin.
Horace dreams of the Bollingen.
Gaius Julius Hyginus fancies the Pulitzer.
Grattius Faliscus wants the MacArthur.
Albius Tibullus hungers for the Lilly.
Sextus Propertius longs for the Nobel.
Marcus Manilius thirsts for the Faber.
Ovid has the jones for the Golden Wreath of Struga.

Gaius Valerius Catullus, for no reason, becomes a giant pillar of fire.

Liber III, Ode 8

Another Feriae Martis and Matronalia, and I'm still a bachelor!
Once again, they make me tread across these hot coals on the
Grass, bearing flowers, an onion, and a little kettle of incense
Hung on my ear. Let's hear it for the Greek and Roman rituals.

After that huge pine fell and just about poleaxed me, I vowed
A big goat and feast to Bacchus every year. That's why I'm still
Unmarried. Or so the priestesses say. There are temples hidden
Underground, and many libraries, too. Aelius is a faint slate blue.

Maecenas, I've got three amphoras of wine from the time of
Tullus. How about we drink a hundred cups to your legionary
Mate at the front, keep the lamps on till dawn, no rancor or
Envy allowed? I'm peeling the pitch and uncorking the first.

Forget, for a spell, caro, your resentments against Augustus.
Cotiso and the Dacians are toast, the Mede are slaughtering
Themselves in civil war, the Cantabriani are finally subdued,
And the Scythians are running like lemmings across the plains.

Think how mysterious your name would be, Maecenas, if
You could follow it to where the first person thought of
Saying it, naming himself that, not in the past but in the
Future. Someone else, centuries from now, shall write this.

Relax, then. You can't do much about the public's opinion.
Take a break. Here's the first cup of one hundred between
Us. We'll have the pleasure of our uncomplicated company.
Stop being so damn anxious and serious all the time, friend!

Liber III, Ode 30

My rivals may not like it, but these odes I'm making will last
Longer than titanium. The great pyramids crumble... No
Millennia of rain, nor withering storms, nor march of empires
Can erode them. I'll die, but not the best of me, peeps.

Even their fragments will shoot out light in all directions. Not to brag
Too much, but the green patina of translucination, in addition, shall
Deepen the praise. While some far-off Pope opens his cool, Ephesian
Frigidaire, they'll proclaim—where the Aufidus sweeps away

Great rocks, or where Daunus ruled his parched domain—
How I, a commoner from the boondocks, did weave Aeolian music
Into modern, jaw-dropping verse. Forgive this boast, Melpomene, for
The honor just as much, we know, belongs to you. But make it new, now,

The laurelled crown from Apollo. Put its synthetic leaves on my head.
And I will say to the envious cynics, forever: You must change your life.

Liber IV, Ode 1

Oh, so it's poetry war again, Venus, and after this short,
Nice vacation? Maybe give me a bit more time? I'm not
What I was back in hot Cynara's day. Cold goddess of
Agonism, I've grown tired of your bellicose snares.

Maybe someone else? Why not Kentuvius Maximus in his
Big house, for instance? That's the address for some sad
Fun. All his hair's dropped out, though he's still self-righteous,
Always eager to represent the helpless and himself.

He's the boy to carry your triumphant banner wherever
Triumph takes him! And once he's trounced some online
Rival, he'll no doubt put your twenty-foot statue on an
Ochre plinth in a pine grove, by the red shores of Lake Alba…

Young satyrs dancing round your image there will stomp their
Dewy feet in charming Sapphic-time of Salian miniature ponies.
Yes, the waters throw your image back to you, goddess, as
Your body throws its own image on the ground in the sunshine.

Me, I've surrendered all hope of Eros's return. And yet, in dreams,
I follow his dark wings across the Field of Mars, to find her by the
Rushing Tiber. I hold her in my arms, and my eyes well with tears.
I try to wake her, but my mind freezes over, and I cannot speak.

TAVERN JOKES

Poetry Joke 1

The ghost of Henry Kissinger walks into a bar in 2222 and sees the ghost of Zhou Enlai in a booth, nursing a shot and a beer. Kissinger orders a double round and goes over to say hello to his old friend. The ancient men greet each other warmly.

After they've reminisced a bit, in nostalgic mode, Kissinger looks his Marxist friend in the eye and says—

"So, seriously now, Zhou, give me, at long last, your objective assessment of Language writing. Was it, from the vantage point of historical materialism, a good thing or a bad thing, for the progressive development of international poetics?"

Zhou downs a shot, looks at Kissinger, and says, very slowly—

"Well, Henry, even assuming that poetry's internal dialectics ever had anything to do with the greater laws of History, it would be way too early to tell."

Poetry Joke 2

So, there's this little flying machine the color of lapis lazuli, just sitting there in a field.

Pulitzer Prize poet John Gould Fletcher, helmeted and goggled, climbs in.

"I will fly, nonstop, from Oklahoma City to Tulsa!" he declares to one hundred flashing camera bulbs.

Search parties are scouring the barren land.

Poetry Joke 3

So, you know that saying, "If there is smoke, can fire be far behind?"

Well, two days later, deep in the Tongass, an emergency crew finds the burned-out cabin of the ancient hermit, Weldon Kees.

"Hello, boys," he says to them. "I've been waiting for you."

Poetry Joke 4

So, one day, sometime in the mid-1990s, the great poet Tom Raworth steps into a crop circle in the fields of Wiltshire, with a very healthy moustache.

"I swear to Almighty God and the Queen," he exclaims, "I had a moustache when I stepped in, and now it is bloody gone!"

Poetry Joke 5

The infamous, sometimes violent jewel thief, François Villon, sneaks in.

Emily Moore, a younger poet, is weeping away in her girlfriend's arms, babbling that her decision to appear in the anthology AMERICAN HYBRID will haunt her reputation for the rest of her poetic life.

"O God, O God, what have I done," etc. etc.

The intruder turns away. Softly behind him, he closes the door.

Poetry Joke 6

"But why was Frank O'Hara so high up in the flowering chestnut, moaning like a cat?" asks Barbara Guest.

"I don't know," says John Ashbery. "But slowly, hand over hand, young fireman Kenneth climbed the ladder, toward the enigma."

Poetry Joke 7

Some guy walks into a bar and yells, "All poets are assholes!"

Another guy, wearing a beret at the end of the bar, says, "I object to that remark."

The guy responds: "Why? Are you a poet?"

"No, I'm an asshole," says the guy with the beret.

Poetry Joke 8

A grad student in the Writing Arts Program at Brown walks into a bar and sees his friend, also a poet in the Program, sitting there. She has a copy of *Devotions: The Selected Poems of Mary Oliver* in front of her. Oddly, right next to the book is a twelve-inch pianist, playing Chopin on a toy-sized grand piano.

The grad student says to his friend, "What on earth? Why the hell are you reading a book by *Mary Oliver*?!?"

Though that could well be the punchline, it isn't. Because surprisingly, the friend pulls an ancient-looking lamp from her tote bag and tells him the genie inside will grant him one wish.

So the grad-student guy rubs the bottle, and to his amazement, a puff of purple smoke spews out and slowly collects in the form of a genie. In a booming voice, the genie tells the man he has but one wish.

The man thinks and says, "OK, I wish I had a million bucks."

In the blink of an eye, the bar is filled with wild turkeys, gobbling away, flying into customers, standing on top of the bar, dunking their heads into people's drinks.

"My god, what the blistering barnacles just happened?!" the guy shouts out.

His friend replies, "I know. Did you really think I wanted a book by Mary Oliver, accompanied by a 12-inch pianist?"

Poetry Joke 9

A poet walks into a NYC bar with a parrot on his shoulder.

The bartender says, "Where did you get *that?*"

The parrot says, "At the AWP Convention—they're as ubiquitous as pigeons!"

Poetry Joke 10

A poet, a critic, and an MFA student walk into a bar.

They sit down and each starts reading *My Life*, by Lyn Hejinian.

The bartender literally spits on the ground and shouts, "Get your sorry, no good, goddamned asses out of here. We don't serve Language poets and never will—not after the way you treated Tom Clark in the late 80s!"

Poetry Joke 11

A poet walks into a bar and says to the bartender: "I'll have a Gin and ... // ... Tonic."

The bartender smirks and asks, "Why the big pause, guy?"

The poet says, "Because I'm a poet. And it's not a pause, jerkoff, it's a caesura. Now give me my ... // ... fucking drink."

Poetry Joke 12

A dangling participle breaks free from a lost poem by Kenneth Koch and walks into a bar.

Enjoying a cocktail and chatting with Barbara, the mysterious evening passes pheasantly.

Poetry Joke 13

Sappho walks into a bar in North Dakota.

"What'll it be, cutie?" says the barkeep.

"Rosy-fingered dawn," says Sappho.

"This is a cowboy bar, ma'am. We don't serve fancy drinks here," says the barkeep.

Sappho glares at him. "You burn me."

"Never heard of that one, either. What is it, one of those flaming cocktails? Look, how about a nice cold can of Bud?"

"Oh, for crissakes, fine," says Sappho. "Just give me a damn can of Bud. I'm hotter than hell."

Poetry Joke 14

An infinite number of poets walk into a bar. The bar is called The Place, located in Purgatory. The first four who belly up are Robert Duncan, Helen Adam, Robin Blaser, and Jack Spicer. The infinite number of other poets wait behind them, all with reverential expression and bearing.

"What'll it be, you lovely people?" says the bartender.

"I'll have a pint of Pliny the Elder," says Robert Duncan, "easy on the foam."

"I'll have a snifter of Oban Single Malt from Scotland," says Helen Adam, "three fingers, one cube."

"I'll have a glass of milk and a straw," says Robin Blaser, "with a shot of Knob's Creek on the side."

"And I'll have an infinite number of bottles of Anchor Steam" says Jack Spicer, "for my ghost friends behind me, here, who send me endless broken radio messages, even in the afterlife. And because infinity has no limit, that means I will have an infinite number of Steams left over for myself, even after I distribute an infinite number to my ghost pals. Those infinite beers left over for me should last me the length of my death…"

"That's an awful lot of beers," says the bartender.

"Serve 'em up, you beautiful boy," says Jack. "And give me one extra for my homey Lorca, who's right behind me."

Poetry Joke 15

Verlaine walks into an elegant bar and orders a drink. Though no one knows it yet in Paris, the infamous poète-maudit—writer of beloved, crystalline alexandrines—has shot Rimbaud in the arm, in Brussels, three days before. Their love affair is done. The bartender returns in his coat and tie and sets the drink down before him, with practiced flair.

"And how is my dearest poet on this fine night of full moon and stars?" he says.

Verlaine doesn't answer. He glares at the drink for almost five minutes, gets up without touching it, and storms out, sobbing, shouting horrible curses.

The bourgeois clientele hardly even notices. They're both used to it and drunk on absinthe. They've come to know, and accept, that poets will be poets.

Fifteen minutes later, Verlaine walks calmly back into the bar with a strange smile on his face. He stops in the middle of the large room.

For some reason, he has swapped his previous felt bowler for an Eton cap, popular among Communards, two years before. Slowly, he reaches into his inside coat pocket.

"I SAID I WANTED A FULL TWIST OF LEMON, NOT A GODDAMN SPANISH OLIVE! he bellows, shattering with a single bullet the great mirror in the martini bar of the Hotel Corbeil.

Poetry Joke 16

John Ashbery walks into a bar after a reading in Iowa City. It's 1995. He orders a Dirty Martini. The bartender, a bit drunk from tippling on the sly, says, "You are my favorite poet, Mr. Ashbery. If you will write down, on this paper napkin, a 'two or three guys walk into a bar' joke right off the top of your head and sign it for me, I will make you the damndest, dirtiest martini you ever did sip in your 60-some years."

So Ashbery takes out his pen and knocks off three sentences:

"Two were alive. One came round the corner / clipclopping [sic]. Three were the saddest snow ever seen in Prairie City."

The bartender looks at the napkin and says, "Huh? You mean the guy's a horse? What kind of joke is that?"

Poetry Joke 17

A poet walks into a bar down the street from the Poetry Project. He has a dog on a leash. The bartender, himself a regular at the Project, says, "Get that dirty dog out of here!" And the guy says, "Hey, camerado, wait, my dog knows all about poetry, and he can talk…"

The bartender says, "If your dog talks about poetry, I'll give you $500 your choice of booze for a fortnight. If your dog *doesn't* talk, I'll throw you both through a window."

"You're on," the guy says, and turns to his dog:

"Ben Jonson, what do you call the top of a building?" The dog goes, "Roof!" The guy says, "Ben Jonson, what do you call the top of your mouth?" The dog goes, 'Roof!" The guy says, "Ben Jonson, what's the greatest poetry press or journal of all time?" The dog goes, "Roof!"

The bartender then picks the two of them up and throws them through a window. The dog shakes it off, looks at his owner and says, in a pitch-perfect Brooklyn twang:

"You think I should have said *Fuck You / A Magazine of the Arts*?"

Poetry Joke 18

Gaius Valerius Catullus walks into a bar, raises two fingers, and shouts at Caelius Rufus, the bartender and his rival for Lesbia:

HEY, YOU, WHORE BOY OF CICERO... FIVE BEERS.

Poetry Joke 19

A poet in her late fifties walks into a bar. She orders a glass of wine. The bartender sets it down in front of her, and she puts her head down on the table and begins to weep. Deep, quiet sobs and shaking.

"Are you OK," says the bartender. "What's wrong?"

The poet gathers herself, sort of...

"Oh, I don't know," she says. "I just spent four or five hours at the conference and didn't talk to a single soul, except people staffing tables at the Book Fair. You know, I've tried so hard, and I've been trying for such a long time. I feel I've got so much to say, but when I go to write, nothing comes out the way I feel it. I've wanted so badly to be admired for my writing, but no one is interested, nobody cares. Rejection after rejection. And I go to these conferences, and all these successful poets are there, they seem so happy. And I just kind of sit there, off to the side, watching, like I did in high school, when I could at least console myself that I would become a prizewinning poet and show them, in the end. And now, here I am, nearing that end, with nothing. Oh, I'm so sorry to put this on you, I'm really embarrassed! I'll be OK. I apologize, really..."

"I wish I knew what to say," says the bartender. "I don't know anything about poetry. But I'm pretty sure most of those poets who seem so happy and successful to you aren't so happy and successful. I mean, I'm sure there are lots of poets who feel the same way you do—people who try really hard and no one sees them. And they have times when they cry too, I'll bet..."

"Yes, thank you, you're right," says the poet. "I do appreciate your listening to me. You seem like such a kind person. Thank you."

And so the poet sits there for about an hour, alone, nursing her one glass of wine, half-reading a prizewinning book she bought at the fair. Then she pays her tab and walks back to her hotel.

THE CLOUDS, THE BIRDS, THE FROGS

The Armored Train

I never liked the Seahawks. I came to Spokane four years ago, and I've tried, but I'm still a Packers fan.

I've never been invited to read in Seattle. But that's OK. I have a phobia of flying and the armored train that goes across the pass is unreliable in winter.

Once I took it to attend an Open Reading at a coffee shop there. I mean in Seattle. But chugging up Snoqualmie Pass, the antique engine couldn't push its great plow through the blizzard. All us poets on the poetry train were jovial about it. We just read amazing experimental poems to each other as the train disappeared under the snows.

Things went from bad to worse. The Budweiser ran out and then the $4 yogurts and the Pop-Tarts, too. After a few weeks, we began to eat the weaker ones. Then it was time to draw straws. Some poets went mad, tunneled up the snow with spoons, and crawled off across the crust, never to be found. The great spruces loomed. Yet thanks be to God, the Merciful One, the following May saw record heat, and the train roofs began to peek through the snows.

From the stinking observation car, poets cheered, as the helicopters circled around, looking for a place to land. But like the Uruguayan poet Alcira Soust Scaffo, in the *Savage Detectives*, I hid in the filthy toilet because I have a phobia of flying. Plus, I didn't want to deal with the scandal of poetry cannibalism, which soon covered all the newspapers by the cash registers at WalMart. Let them believe I was one of the weaker ones who was eaten, I thought, again and again, until I started chanting it out loud, through my freezing snot and tears, as I struggled through the twenty-foot drifts, like Doctor Zhivago, towards the beautiful City on the Sound.

When I stumbled into North Bend, I knew I would make it in time for one of the June Open Mic readings, at the coffeeshop in Seattle, only forty miles away. I went to the North Bend Corner Café, where scenes from Twin Peaks had been filmed. There was the laughing face of the man who murdered his own daughter on the wall, to prove it. I was famished. I had an actual non-poet steak and mashed potatoes. I bought some khakis, a tweed jacket, a beautiful shirt, a tie, and a pipe, like the pipe Alan Tate used to smoke, the one in that painting by Magritte. The poems I still had in my pocket were what they used to call "Language" poems, full of references to China.

Eftsoons, a week later, I was in the shadow of the Great Needle Tower. No one recognized me at the Open Reading. Nervously, I went to the podium and began. I said I had just moved to the city and was looking for a place to stay the night. The other poets there, all five of them, gave me a standing ovation at the end. I began to weep.

One of them came up to me for a donation and asked if I wanted to go out back and smoke some meth. I said, No, no thank you, Alice, but I'll have a Pop-Tart over here at the table, and also some snow water in that plastic bottle.

OK, she said, go ahead and be anti-social, if you want. But FYI, it's not going to get you very far in the poetry world around *these* parts, asshole.

Dog Petting

My dog's name is Ben Jonson. My own name is Kent Johnson, and I write poetry and sometimes theatrical prose, so I thought it was very clever of me to name my dog Ben Jonson. One day, my dog was lying in the family room, with his four paws up in the air. I was sitting next to him, scratching his chest up and down. He started panting, so I scratched even harder to please him more. As I sped up my hand, I noticed that my left leg began to lift and pump the air. It felt good, so I scratched my dog's chest even faster. My leg was now pumping terrifically fast, my whole-body tingling in this ecstatic sort of way. By and by, my dog was panting with such intensity, he began to gag, as if he had just eaten a hot bowl of grass for breakfast. Then my dog composed himself, stood up, and with his tongue all over my neck, mouth, and face, he communicated that I had better lie down on my back instantly, or else. I obeyed my Master. Then, because he is a southpaw, he placed his padded left foot on the center of my chest and began to rub. He rubbed in slow, tender circles at first, picking up speed, but little by little, patiently, almost imperceptibly. Time vanished in the sweetness of it, until I realized with a start that he was suddenly rubbing my chest in small, hard circles, at a very high velocity. He began to bark incoherently at me, as if he were saying dirty dog words. Strangely, and even though my legs were spread and up in the air, they were comfortable and still, and a great feeling of tranquility fell over me. But the right hind leg of my dog, whose front paw was pleasuring me, was now pumping at a great velocity, just as mine had been when our positions were reversed. Faster and faster in a kind of madness went his hind leg. I could also tell you that he had a very noticeable erection, something which male dogs get for no apparent reason, but that would be too much information, and you likely would not believe it, in any case. But let's say he did and that this made me feel, shall we say, a bit uncomfortable. I stood up on my two legs. OK, that's enough, Ben Jonson, let's go for a walk, I sternly said. He looked at me and started to growl. Yeah, yeah, he snarled, Walk, a-walka, walka-doodle the cute half poodle. I'm tired of walking you, Kent Johnson. Lie back down here, and let's have some fun... Hey! Watch your mouth, young man, or I'll wash it out with soap! I yelled. Go to your man-cave kennel, and I mean like right this very second!!

He hung his handsome head, sadly, and walked very slowly to his man-cave.

Poema Político

—a Roque Dalton

"But that's life in the tropics," as an FMLN guerrilla said to me one day, in almost perfect English, recovering in Managua from a serious shrapnel wound to his hip, at the working-class *hospedaje* in Managua where I was staying, in 1983, which a bunch of Honduran guerrillas were staying at, too, while on leave from training with the FSLN forces in Jinotega, against the CIA-managed Contras.

I got into drunk shouting matches with a few of the main men and women from that contingent almost every night at the corner *comedor*, over Victoria beers, debating the unfolding events of the Solidarity movement in Poland. I defended Solidarity; they thought it was an imperialist plot. We loved each other. I even slept with one of the women Comandantes who would yell at me, with tears in her eyes. I am not making that up. It was wonderful sex.

What are you reading she said to me once, on the patio. It's a book of poems by Frank O'Hara, I said. He's an American poet. Oh, she said. Would you read me some? It's in English, I said. I understand that, asshole, she said, Do I really look so dense to you? Read me a poem by this O'Haris... O'Hara, I said. Does it matter? she said. And so, I read her "A Step Away from Them," even though she couldn't understand a single word. But she listened with her eyes closed the whole time. That was a beautiful poem, she said, opening her eyes.

Soon they would all be killed (or else tortured and disappeared in mass graves after capture) in a U.S. counterinsurgency campaign when they returned to Honduras to try to do what the Sandinistas did in Nicaragua. The handsome young guy from El Salvador went back to the front in Chalatenango and got killed, as well.

Those were the days.

Strange, it occurs to me now that if I'd read her a poem by Kenneth Koch, instead, a long one, say, like "The Circus II," that everything would have been different, that every moment in her life would have been altered in slight ways, leading to cascading changes in her experience, including to her not getting killed, while holding out in a bakery, in a small village, somewhere. Or if I'd kept her there for hours, intoning my way through Ashbery's *Three Poems*, maybe she'd be living in Cuba, now, or Cleveland, doting on seven grandkids.

I know I'm not saying any of this in a sufficiently "poetic" form for a political poem. Sorry about that… I started out with the best of intentions, but it seems I just can't get it going, or maybe it's that I've tried to keep it going for way too long.

A political poem should be written in verse, I suppose, not in flat prose. But that's life in the tropics, sometimes it just wants to be prose, you know?

And to say that what's done, Beatriz, though that was not your real name, is now done.

Ekphrasistically

in memoriam, James Agee

Ever since I was a senior in high school, I've had the desire to write ekphrastic poems.

I never did. I hope this is an ekphrastic poem, but maybe other poets will say it isn't.

Well, perhaps, reading this, wherever you are, and in whatever time, you are not a poet. Hopefully for you (and for me), you are not.

So, ekphrastic poems are ones about paintings, in case you didn't know. If you didn't, don't feel bad: For from my senior year in high school, until I was a second-year graduate student in Poetry Studies at the University of Wisconsin/Milwaukee, I was sure the adjectival form of ekphrasis was "ekphrasistic," with two i's, and I always used to wonder to myself how the descriptive word for poems written in description of paintings sounded like some sort of psychiatric pathology suffered by poets who are terrified by the world.

In fact, I once gave a paper at a regional literature conference in Iowa City (a big deal for me, because it was my first conference paper ever, and also because I was just returning from four months at St. Elizabeth's), and it was a paper titled, "Ekphrasistic Splendor: Poems of Second-Generation New York School Poets Under the Influence of John Ashbery's 'Self-Portrait in a Convex Mirror.'"

And while reading that paper, I pronounced "ekphrastic" as "ekphrasistic" no fewer than twenty-two times, wondering, as I neared the end of the presentation, why the dozen or so people in the room were either 1) whispering to each other, 2) looking at the floor in embarrassment, or 3) visibly snickering. This would have been May of 1985.

That night I got stinking drunk by myself at a dive bar called Poet's Oblivion (only in Iowa City), where I seemed to be the only person under fifty-five, in its bluish light. I went back to my Motel 6 room and cried myself to sleep.

The next morning, around eleven, I got up, feeling rather strange. It seemed like the right thing to do, so I shaved my face, chest, legs, and pubic hair, and went to McDonald's, waiting on foot in the drive thru, in a line of cars, because I was too mortified to go inside anywhere, afraid that I'd be seen by someone who'd been at my panel.

Much less did I wish to go back to the small, regional conference at the Student Union, sure that everyone there by now knew what a pathetic, know-nothing loser I really was. How is it possible, I thought, standing in the drive-thru line, that for seven or eight years, despite reading lots of essays in relation to ekphrastic poetry, I thought I was reading essays in relation to "ekphrasistic" poetry? It didn't help that the teenagers in the Chevy pickup immediately behind me were extravagantly mocking me, this dumbass street-person cad, carrying a pile of poetry books, standing in a long line of cars, in the drive-through at McDonald's...

I'll take an Egg McMuffin and a cup of coffee, I said, my voice shaking, to the girl with the headset and the long, tangled morning glory vines trailing out of her bright blue eyes. It took forever, it seemed, to get my order, and cars began to honk, spelling out my four-lettered name in repeated morse code, replacing the E with a U.

I was feeling very lightheaded by now, sort of how I always felt at St. Elizabeth's, after the sessions with the gauze stuffed between my teeth, so I went across the parking lot to a flowering tree of some kind and climbed into its lower branches. There I perched, hidden by beautiful blossoms from the ugly world, eating my Egg McMuffin and drinking my coffee. People driving or walking by seemed to be looking at me and pointing, but I knew it was just my nervous and vulnerable state of mind, the aftermath of what I'd been through the previous evening.

I climbed down from the white, flaming tree and without even remembering how I got there, I walked through the seven-mile-high diamond entrance of the University of Iowa Fine Arts Museum.

I asked a guard with a black Japanese helmet and armor where the paintings were. From behind his mask, he said that they were all around me and always would be, for there was no escaping Representation, until I chose to vanish into its hidden, manifold Chambers. You are, he said, in a Japanese accent, standing in one of the finest university collections of tromp l'œil paintings in the whole damn country.

He was right, there they were, astonishing paintings from Flanders and Holland all around me. I walked up to one with a golden frame wider on every side than the canvass itself, with a terrified little boy climbing out of it, grasping the golden perimeter, as if climbing from a window—but a window posing as a painting that was pretending to pretend to not be itself, neither in the "Past," from which it seemed to have come, nor even now, in a continuous, back-gazing "Future," tenuously posing as a "Present." This boy, with his goggle eyes and open mouth, looked to be three-dimensional, coming out into the Actual World Itself!!

The work was from the 19th century, and it was titled "Escaping Criticism" (a title much shorter than that of my paper), by Pere Borrell del Caso. I was transfixed by this painting, and I was silent before it, for what seemed like hours. I felt hunger, so I took the last of the McMuffin from my pocket and ate it.

And as I did, I realized, with a feeling of utter disbelief for which I have no words, that the face of the boy was the exact face of one of my dearest heroes, the great poet and non-fiction documentarian James Agee, who died so young! Yes, the frightened boy was the spitting image of the 13-year-old James Agee, in the famous photograph taken right after he has won the Yale Younger Poets Award, in 1933. The almost-child looked straight at me.

I know how you feel, he said, sotto voce. Having come out here to meet you, I suddenly feel the same, as you can see from my face. You may be wondering why I have come so close, like a sun, who is burning your gentle skin? I have travelled so far and have done this for you.

But James Agee, I cried. You have been dead for thirty years!

Yes, of course, he replied. That is why I am here. There is no reason now to be afraid. It is much safer inside, far back, in the hidden chambers, where there is no Representation. No one to judge or demean you, not even yourself. The Museum Guard in the samurai armor whom you spoke to was pointing the way...

And so, I slowly disrobed, until I was naked and hairless as the day I was born. And I took the hand of my friend, and I climbed, ekphrasistically, into the painting.

I Once Met Robert Hogg

for Bob Hogg, on his 80th birthday

I once met the magnificent poet, Robert Hogg. This was in 1965, at Onetto's Supper Club, in Buffalo. I was only seven years old, and Bob was 23. He was talking to some other grad students at the bar. I went up to the bar stool beside him and climbed up. Hey, kiddo, he said, his arms weirdly curved around eight salt and pepper shakers, as if he were protecting them from the coming disaster that would befall American poetry, in about a dozen years. You look a little worse for wear, youngster, he said. I looked right through him because I wanted to be a tough guy. Bob was taken aback by my glare, it seemed, and looked away. The bartender came over in his white jacket and black tie. What'll it be, tiny soldier, he asked me. Make it a double scotch, straight up, with a glass of water on the side and a Falstaff for a chaser, I growled. Well, well, said Bob, turning towards me again, what do we have here, a little drinker, huh? I ignored him, emptied my scotch in one take, and took out my spanking new copy of Charles Olson's *Human Universe*, just out. OHO! Shouted Bob. A little boy with a chip on his alcoholic shoulder who also reads essays by Charles Olson! Tell me, guy, are you some kind of poet? By now, all of Bob Hogg's fellow-student friends were looking at me, laughing, and my chronic social anxiety began to take over. I tried to focus on *Human Universe*, but I grew increasingly self-conscious and nervous, and I knew they could tell I really wasn't who I wanted them to see me as. Hey, buster, I'll bet you're probably packing heat, too, eh? said Bob, shaking some pepper on my head. Everyone started to laugh, including the bartender, and I began to cry. I cried, because I wanted to be a poet so bad, just like the young Bob Hogg, who at that time was a grownup to me, and who I knew also knew Olson himself and also Jack Clarke, both of them heroes of mine, even back then, when I was seven. I cried and cried. Then Bob, I will never forget this, put his arm around my shoulder, and sweetly said, There, there, my little friend. Everything will be alright, just as long as you don't become a poet. The best advice I can give you is to put away that book and never look at it again. It's Black Magic… Thank you, Mr. Hogg, I whimpered. You are a very nice and good-looking gentleman. I'd been thinking the same thing, to be honest. Poetry has really only brought pain and loneliness to my life so far! And then, as I wiped away my hot tears, I heard a sudden, booming voice behind me, which shook me to my little bones. I turned around and looked up. IT WAS CHARLES OLSON! Hey, he said, what is this fucking seven-year-old kid doing in my chair for crissakes? Can a poet not even have his own seat at Onetto's anymore? Scram you little munchkin and get to bed, now. But… oh, wait… what's this, OK, said Olson. Seriously? You are READING MY ESSAYS? Well, well, now, hold on, let's have a chat here about this. What are you drinking, kid? Scotch? Hey, Jack, a Macallan for the boy, here, on my tab. So, sit on my knee here, son, and let me tell you a little story about a guy named Maximus of Gloucester… I sat on Charles Olson's knee and looked at Bob, and Bob gave me a wink, and said (mouthing it, slowly and silently):

Don't tell me I didn't warn you, tough guy. But it's too late now.

Perry's Nut House: A Ghost Story

I love Perry's Nut House. It's a hundred-year-old tourist trap, on Rt. 1, right outside Belfast, Maine.

There are very large, sculpted models of exotic creatures out front, most famously an elephant. Inside, there are many stuffed animals and funhouse mirrors, too, which make people look like they've been stretched thin or squashed fat. There's one where your head becomes huge and your body becomes tiny; in another, your head becomes tiny, and your body becomes huge.

In the cellar, at the entrance to a labyrinth, there is an illusion called The Eternity View, which makes it seem you're reproduced in an endless, repeating series, forever into the past. But it's really two big parallel mirrors reflecting one another, along with whatever is inside them, infinitely, at the speed of light. One time, down there, I looked at my endless selves receding, tinier and tinier, until I couldn't see myself. I knew I was there, far back, but I was also gone. Like someone just outside the frame of an old photo, who is there and yet not there... I was eleven, looking at myself repeating without end. I felt strange and began to cry. My father worked there summers as a teenager.

It's a tad off topic, but a bit down the road is Bucksport, where the image of a life-size, female-looking leg adorns the gravestone of Captain Buck, the early 19th century town Founder. He was a wicked drunk who shattered his wife's right leg by throwing her down the mansion stairs, causing its need for amputation. Back then they used those big saws you see in the movies. People drink a lot of whiskey, bite down on a stick, and the surgeon saws. Shortly thereafter, she died of gangrene, her last words being, they say, an oath that she would haunt her evil seadog of a husband for all time.

Captain Buck died the following month, while his schooner was docked in Portland, offloading salted cod. It was a large crate of cod that dropped upon his head. Fare thee well, Captain Fuck, mumbled the crewmembers, who despised him greatly. The rope attached to the crate was cleanly cut, but no one told on anyone. So that was the end of Captain Buck, known by his crew, as I just said, as Captain Fuck.

All this is true: The morning after the bad man was buried back in Bucksport's graveyard, the faint, but perfect outline of a woman's shapely leg, as if coming from inside the marble, appeared on the obelisk above his grave. No one could understand it, as the marble had been unblemished, of perfect quality, cut in the deep quarry outside Rockport, from whence the finest marble in all of New England came. The townspeople tried to sand the weird image off, because who wants a human leg on the expensive tomb of their town Founder? After sanding for hours, the strange leg seemed to have been erased, and each person retired to their home, used the chamber pot, doused the candles and lamps, and put their sleeping caps on.

But, lo, the next morning, what do you imagine they found? Eyuh, you guessed it: The female-looking leg had returned! And this time, its outline was yet more apparent, still clearly part of the stone itself, not an image drawn upon it. Again, and with some creeping apprehension, the workers sanded and sanded, and then they retired to their horse-hair beds, once again.

You probably know where this is going. Yes, the leg was back the next morning and with such clear outline, now, that it could not / would not, be sanded off. Try and try as the stonemasons might… It was soon understood by all the townspeople and in the Waldo county villages beyond, that a curse of some kind had been cast upon despicable Captain Buck's tomb, and no one now dare approach the tainted grave.

Anyway, the years went by as they do, and the mysterious, disembodied leg stayed just where it was and became part of the historical scenery and lore of the Penobscot Bay surround. So much so that Perry's Nut House, whose fate you are probably wondering about, since I got a bit sidetracked there, began to sell postcards of Captain Buck's haunted obelisk to summer tourists from out of state, many of whom would then drive down the road to see the apparition for themselves, some posing for gay photographs beside it, before continuing onto whatever other ghostly things awaited them in their lives. My father took a polaroid of me and my two brothers, as children, sitting in front of the obelisk, squinting into the sun. I wish I had that, so I could insert it, in the W.G. Sebald style, after this paragraph. Surely my dad rang up some of those postcards at Perry's, back in the 1940s. He worked the cash register in the mornings, and the candy and soda counter in the afternoons. My mother, a year behind my dad at school, would often come with her friends and sit and sip on their fizzy sodas. My dad would slip them free candy, with a couple extra pieces for my mom. He wore a white shirt and black tie, with one of those paper-boat sanitation hats. My pretty mom would giggle with her young friends and pretend she had not a whit of interest in my dad. World War II was raging, far away, millions of people dying, losing their legs, etc. But there was my smiling father in his paper hat, my giggling young mother, the countless candy jars, the standing, angry bear and the seven-foot moose, the two-headed ewe, the whoopee cushions, the X-Ray spectacles, the rubber reptiles, the funhouse mirrors…

And in the darker cellar beneath, the Maze of Mysteries, where for a nickel you could get lost, maybe even steal a kiss between the parallel mirrors of the Eternity View, to piped-through music, from a vintage pianola.

Seven Smashed Poet Faces

for Kenneth Koch

My name is Kent Johnson, and Kenneth Koch is one of my favorite poets. And one of my favorite poems by Kenneth Koch is "You Were Wearing." It's a poem of youthful courting, an odd poem and very sweet, with quirky details about the clothes and accoutrements the innocent youths were, and now forever are, wearing: an "Edgar Allan Poe printed cotton blouse," a "John Greenleaf Whittier hair clip," a pair of "George Washington, Father of our Country, shoes." The young girl's mother serves tea in "Herman Melville"-themed cups; the father suddenly appears, with a "Dick Tracy necktie." The young sweethearts, wanting some privacy, then go out on the front porch, where they sit on the "Abraham Lincoln swing." The girl sits on the "mouth part," the boy sits on the "knees."

But the best lines are the last two:

"In the yard across the street we saw a snowman holding a garbage can lid / smashed into a likeness of the mad English King, George the Third."

Those lines have haunted me for many years, though I do not know wherefore.

Incidentally, I am not an artist, I am a poet. Why? I think I would rather be an artist, but I am not. Well, for instance, John Ashbery was starting an assemblage. I dropped in. "Sit down on the Anne Bradstreet swing and have a drink" he said. I drank; we drank. I was sitting on the mouth of Anne Bradstreet part and John was sitting on her knees. I looked up. "You have a GARBAGE CAN LID in it." "Yes, it needed something there." "Oh," I said. "Could I have another drink? I have an idea coming on. I'd like to grease the gears."

It was on that tipsy evening—walking home, me unbuttoned all over my previous life, a kid tied to a lamppost, an existence scant in comparison to this one, though not by much—that it dawned on me I could be an artist, even as I was primarily a poet. What I needed was a good Idea, a Concept, one no one else had ever quite thought of before. I wasn't thinking about painting (because painting, as everyone knows, is over), but rather of sculpture in the expanded field, or something, that sort of thing. And now, with a feeling of Zarathustra-like triumph, I knew what Idea I was going to have.

Yes, I would do something that not even my enemy, the creepy poseur Andy Warhol, had thought of, or at least not yet. He or his frienemie Jasper Johns might think of it any minute, of course, or some groupie on their respective art assembly lines might, so there was no time to waste. I literally jogged to the hardware store and asked where the metal garbage-can lids section was. The clerk said that they didn't sell metal garbage can lids separately and that I would need to buy the whole metal can if I wanted a lid. "OK," I said, "where is the metal garbage CAN section, please?" "You're standing in it," he said. And sure enough, there I was, with metal garbage cans and their shield-like lids lined-up all the way down to the end of aisle.

"I'll take all of them," I said. "What do you mean, all of them," he said, "there's like seventy garbage cans here, that's a lot of cash." "That's OK," I said, "I was just hired as a curator at the Museum of Modern Art and got a big fat starting bonus," I said. "What the hell are you going to do with seventy garbage cans?" he said. "Well," I said, putting my hand on my waist and replying in a tone that was both feminine and tough, "even though it's none of your beeswax, I am going to change the Art World, baby."

It is important that I not go on for too long; if I do so, this prose poem will become a short story, and I am not a fiction writer, I am a poet. So, I will get right to the point. Once the garbage cans arrived on the hardware store delivery truck, I carried the stacked cans and lids inside. So long, dining room and balcony! I took off the lids and hung four of them up on the living room wall, just like paintings, except round ones. Then I realized, what am I going to do with all these cans? Because I didn't need them, I spent twenty minutes carrying the new, shiny cans outside. I felt stupid for having lugged them inside in the first place, but it was good exercise, anyway. I stacked one inside the other in a dozen groups and put them out on the curb, as Irony would choose, for the garbage truck.

I regarded the four lids on the wall. I said to myself out loud: "Lids, you will be Art. Just as the wood never dreamed it would become a violin, so you have never dreamed you would be smashed into the face of a famous poet. Each of you, along with your waiting brethren, will bear the image of a famous poet, and be lined up in serial fashion, like Campbell Soup Cans, or metal boxes in Marfa, Texas. You will be coveted by collectors and hung on the walls of museums. Let us begin!" I called out to the lids.

Beneath the first lid in the row of four, I pasted some masking tape, and wrote the name "Kenneth Koch" with a green marker, for how could I not honor the poet who had given me the idea in the first place? I began tentatively, tapping at where the eyes would be. I made two hollows and then I angled my hammer to make the ridge of his brow. The nose was more difficult, for to get its shape I had to strike harder. Sometimes I struck too hard, and I had to take the lid from the wall and tap from behind. Doing this, I realized that the best way to make the nose, the mouth, and the chin was, indeed, to tap or hammer strongly from behind. I also realized that I would need a couple or three chisels of different size to create the hair, the dimple beneath the nose, and especially the ears.

I hammered at Koch's face for around three days. I was done. I stepped back and regarded my work, and I was pleased. Why, Kenneth Koch's face was so lifelike, it almost looked like one of those amazing photo-realist portraits by Chuck Close. I was very happy. I had a six pack of Genesee and some pretzels, admiring my garbage can lid, smashed into an uncanny likeness of the wild American poet, Kenneth Koch.

But there was no time to lose. Andy Warhol was still there, scheming, as always, and so was Jasper Johns and his third-rate boyfriend Robert Rauschenberg, even. I jumped up and approached the second lid, taking a swig from a fifth of Wild Turkey. Beneath the lid, I put some masking tape and wrote the name "Emily Dickinson." I began to work as before, tapping gently, now with force, sometimes wailing at the lid when a deep indentation was required. I stepped back and regarded my work. I could barely believe my eyes.

Though from up close it seemed that I was creating a fine likeness of Emily Dickinson, from a standard viewing distance it didn't look like Emily Dickinson at all. In fact, the smashed face was a kind of mash up, a combination of sort of Gertrude Stein at the top, and a fifteen-year-old Ezra Pound at the bottom. And from the right side, it actually looked like a ragged Sylvia Plath at the bottom, and a beady-eyed Marianne Moore in her crazy hat above.

After putting out the failed garbage can lid with the 70 cans and composing myself with a few highballs, I gathered my determination and approached the next lid. On the masking tape I wrote, "Vladimir Mayakovsky," though it took me a few tries to get the last name right. I began to tap and bang. There was a pounding on the apartment floor above, who knows what the problem could have been, but I paid it no mind. I just wailed at that lid in the manner of Russian Futurism. Or maybe more like Italian Futurism. This lid was done fairly fast. And this time I was certain the Mayakovsky was a success. But when I stepped back to view with more perspective, the face was even more of a mess than Dickinson's! It wasn't Mayakovsky, it was a smashed mélange of Stalin, Neruda, and Anne Sexton! I screamed and screamed four-letter words, and the pounding above commenced again. I went over to the couch, lied down, and began to cry.

I disposed of the Mayakovsky lid same as with the first failure, taking it out to the curb. I resolved I would not give up. Beneath the fourth lid I wrote the name "Max Jacob." His face was a simple one, from the photographs I had seen, nothing remarkable about it, like a chauffeur, maybe, and so I felt, despite my growing despair, that I could smash this lid into his bland face just fine. I had a few martinis and started to really go at it, from the front and then from behind, on the floor. I stepped back. "No, no, no, no!!" I cried, "Oh God in heaven No!" There on the floor was not Max Jacob, but the face of Amiri Baraka on the right after a car crash, and of Ed Dorn on the left after a shotgun blast. I went into the bathroom and threw up in the toilet. Then I took Max Jacob disguised as the Emergency Room victims Amiri Baraka and Ed Dorn out to the garbage.

Now I hung four more lids on the wall. Beneath the first one I wrote the name "Charles Olson." I mixed a pitcher of Manhattans and chugged it down without bothering with the stupid, fancy James Bond glass. I began to smash the shiny lid indiscriminately with a great proprioceptive force for about half an hour. I heard someone pounding at my door, but I didn't care, by this point. Go away! I shouted, I am an Artist and I am working!" "Oh yeah? You'll be working at the Brooklyn Jail Art Studio if you don't fucking stop, you artish-smartish prick, it's 3:30 in the morning! My wife and child have the measles, so have some respect!" "Oh, go jump in the lake, bitch," I slurred. The impatient man left, shouting campily that he'd be back with a baseball bat. I looked up. Oh, it was not Charles Olson--no, oh god, it was the forgotten Marya Zaturenska on top and Wallace Stevens on the bottom, with a little hint of the alcoholic John Berryman in the eyes. It was a mess. I took the lid outside, falling down the stairs, and placed it with the other Smashed Poet lids.

Now I was pissed. I snorted some coke and drank a bottle of absinthe without heating it up. Beneath the next lid I wrote, "John Keats." This time I worked more carefully, aiming my swinging hammer at the three lids I was seeing, then pounding it or them strategically with my bloody fists to create the eyes and the pouty mouth. I stepped back, after pausing to throw up all over the carpet. But that was OK, my cat licked some of it up. This time, when I saw that it wasn't the face of Keats but the shattered fragments of a Grecian Urn right out of the impenetrable essay "The Task of the Translator," I started looking for my Glock, which was funny because if I squinted my eyes, the lid bore a faint resemblance to Walter Benjamin's death mask.

Then Jack Spicer came out half the face of Lawrence Ferlinghetti, but upside down, while the other half was like Helen Adams's lover's eyes should fall out.

"Oh well," I said, breaking a front lower tooth on a chisel. Then I passed out.

The next morning, in depression, disgust, and surrender, I started to take all the remaining lids out to the curb, to leave them with all the others, along with the garbage cans I'd stacked up the day before. But everything was gone! There wasn't a shiny garbage can or lid in sight. That's weird,

I thought, because garbage pick-up is on Thursday not Wednesday? Isn't this Wednesday? Well, they must have changed the schedule I said to myself. I stumbled back inside.

After some coffee and the dry heaves, I called John Ashbery on the telephone. I told him I was in bad shape, wouldn't he please come over to sit with me for a while? He said he was really focused-in on his assemblage with the garbage can lid, and that it was a bad time, but that he would come anyway, "because a friend in need is a friend indeed." I more or less cleaned up the vomit from the carpet and waited on my bed.

I cried on dear Ashbery's shoulder for a spell. "There, there," he softly said. He smiled at me with his gapped teeth. "Look," he said, "there is no shame in only having done one garbage can lid poet-portrait. In fact, it is a wonderful achievement; the Koch is an uncanny representation, a work even I am jealous of." Then he pulled out a polaroid of the garbage can lid affixed to his assemblage. "I took it this morning, it is finished."

It was the perfect face at age 32 of C.P. Cavafy! "And I brought along a poem by him to read to you, which might make you feel better, he said. He read me "The First Step," which ends thusly: "To have come this far is no small achievement: what you have done already is a glorious thing."

I dried my tears and blew my nose. "Yes, yes, that is beautiful. I feel better already. Thank you for being my friend, Ash."

"Of course," he said. "You know, it's funny, I saw Robert Rauschenberg last night at Max's, and he said he was preparing a work that had garbage can lids in it, too. He said he was going to show them just as he found them, smashed, ruined lids, he said, with nothing added."

Four days later, I walked into the Phoenix Gallery, on 10th, and saw 300 people gazing in wonder at my failed garbage can lids on the wall, the name of Robert Rauschenberg above the seven objects, in gold letters, with the title of the work beneath:

"Seven Smashed Poet Faces."

As a group, including a long, framed scroll of a tire track hung above, co-made with the mushroom freak John Cage, the price was $100,000, a lot of money for the 1960s.

And it was all marked SOLD.

A Review of James Tate

for Dan Chiasson

The other day I started to read James Tate's posthumous *The Governor's Lake*, subtitled *The Lost Poems*. I liked the book very much. The poems are very nice, they are all in prose, and they meander along, like some forgotten, lost footpath in the Berkshires, which makes the subtitle all the more poignant, and good on the editors for choosing it. The poems tend to launch with clarity and purpose, then drift, before coming to in a fog, far from the blazes of conventional logic or narrative satisfaction. Sorry if it seems I'm overly self-conscious of my prose. A madcap style is the vehicle for implying other, graver things. Iridescent, cretaceous, oyster, cerise, chamois, and more, all of these at once–all words used by Dickinson, in her prime. The jewels are all there; but the real treasure isn't any precious stone, far from it, no. Yes, styles are like trade routes; they fall out of favor, eventually vanish into the sands. But he never cared, and why should he? He rode his loping camel with patient grace and had a flowing headdress to taunt and beat all standard drones. I was reminded, while reading (for what could be more natural than to remember such an occasion?), of the time back in the early 90s, when I visited James Tate in the Berkshires, close to Camp Beckett, where I had worked as a teen. It was really great to meet him, as I had always been a fan of *The Lost Pilot*, which I read when I was at Camp Beckett, actually, and which, again, makes the subtitle all the more poignant–good on the editors for choosing it, as I'd said. It was very nice to meet Dara Wier, too. She is a terrific poet who was James's wife, and because she got her grad degree from lowly Bowling Green State, just like I did, though about a decade earlier than me, it made the encounter extra special. She was very nice, very smart and pleasant, and pointed out this or that species of the many-colored bird-burst at the seven or so feeders they had in the vast and shaded yard: orioles, yellow warblers, goldfinches, purple finches, indigo buntings, spotted towhees, black headed grosbeaks, rose breasted grosbeaks, American redstarts, and the first and only scarlet tanager I have ever seen in my life. What kind of bird seed do you use? I said. The kind that was only made in the lost town of Governor, she said. Where's Governor, I said, I've never heard of it. It's over that hill, over there, straight north, said Dara, and it's been sitting on the bottom of a lake, since the spring of 1897. We got the bags of seed from the last resident-survivor of the town, seven years ago, who happened to be the son of the owner of the town's famous bird seed factory, said James. We inherited about seven-hundred sacks of perfectly exquisite bird seed, said Dara, it keeps forever. The town is sitting on the bottom of a lake? I said. Yep, that is correct, said Dara. It's rumored there are unknown daguerreotypes of Dickinson down there, said James, including two of her sitting on the lap of her Master, locked in glass, owned by an early collector, the town mortician. And scuba divers say that most everything is still perfectly intact, all the old-style business signs on Main Street, and the old houses with their fences and Victorian porches, the school house with its steeple and bell, and the statues of Emerson and Fireside poets frowning in the park of swaying grass beds, he said, pausing from toking on his joint. He looked off over the bluish, smoky hills to the west, with his goat-patch beard and roguish mien. Do you want some grass, he said. No thanks, I said, but thank you for asking, it makes me hallucinate, I'm already seeing an impossible number of songbirds from second hand smoke. Ha ha ha ha ha, Dara and he both laughed for what seemed like seven minutes, or so, until the echoes of their guffaws started to come back, resounding in weird concussions, like ghosts from the hills. Hey, said Dara, wiping her eyes, why don't you and Kent take a hike up Governor's Hill so he can see the lake that covers the lost town like a sheet of glass, ha ha? Sure, said James, ha. So we did. James was tired; he couldn't get out of his chair. So I strapped him to my back with some belts, which he didn't seem to mind, his arms were still free, and he somehow managed, even though we were back to back, as it were, to unhinge his arms from his sockets so that he could stroke my hair, backwards, and he did so for the whole duration of the arduous climb up the hill, softly crooning, in a gravelly voice, There, there, my dear boy, there, there... We will soon achieve the top, do not falter... And, no, of course, falter I did not: The dazzling, emerald lake with the lost town hidden beneath its glass top spread out beneath us, perfectly still and silent, though it was not that large, more like a pond, it seemed to me, though maybe my judgment was off. Isn't it totally neat, said James. Yes, it is really some fucking view, I said. There is a lost species of humpbacked trout in that lake, said James. Wow, I said, really? That's amazing. And then, after a while of my laboriously turning this way and that so that James could also appreciate the vista and comment on it, we headed back down the mountain, though this time James made me strap him to my front, which made it very awkward, perilous, even, to go downhill. But because he was now strapped around my groin, he was able to use his long, simian arms like a pair of extra legs, keeping us, at least, from tumbling down the slippery rocks. Good job, poet! he said, when we finally got back to the gingerbread house from whence we'd come, where he and Dara lived on the weekends, or when they were on seven-year sabbaticals every four years from U of Mass/ Amherst. Four legs are always better than two in poetry, though we are like two peas in a pod! he said. Dara was up on the grass roof, in a gauze white dress, helping one of the goats to give birth to Siamese goats, and it didn't seem to be going easy. Did you have a good time? she said above the heartbreaking squeals to heaven. There's goat meat and beans on the stove, just help yourselves! Yes, dear, we had a great time, said James, unstrapping himself from my body, then leading me like a boyfriend by the hand into the gingerbread house. And it is only just now, right at the point where I go into the house, when the plot about the lost lake and the lost pilot and the lost book was totally ready for takeoff, that I realize, looking by chance at the cover of the book again, that the subtitle is not *LOST Poems*. It is *LAST Poems*. *Last Poems*! OMG! All that climb up the ancient basalt or maybe granite hill, whatever, just to pretend like we were flying over The Governor Lake like ghosts or birds or drones. And not only that. The title of the goddamn book is *The Government Lake*, not *The Governor's Lake*. So now none of this book review even makes any damn sense, or is too embarrassing to share. Geez and shoot me now with a blunderbuss. Yes, depressing and a wasted trip, you could say. But even so, I do have to share: Those chunks of goat meat and ranch beans still taste in my mouth-thoughts like the sweetest kisses of Esmeralda. I mean, you tell me, poets, truly. What are the chances, eh?

A Dream Review

of John Bradley's Spontaneous Mummification, Winner of the
2019 International James Tate Poetry Prize, Dublin, Ireland

for Matt Zapruder

Three hundred years ago, when the Earth was still living, I wrote a dream review of James Tate's *The Government Lake: Last Poems.*

I had dreamt there that I carried Tate in his chair up the mount, strapped to my back, to look down at the teal sheen of Government Lake, shrouding its drowned 19th century village beneath. And then, after a smoke and a spell at the top, I carried him back down the same way we'd come up, though now he was strapped to my strong, thirty-something abdomen, while he used his long, mantis arms as spindle-brakes, to keep us from tumbling down the path.

At last, the shack appeared, glowing, on the twilit clearing, where Dara Wier was waiting. We all kicked back on the busted porch, on ripped-up Packard Predictor seats. And there, he read me his last poems, in manuscript, by the wick of a Coleman lamp.

But now James Tate was dead. I said to John Bradley, *What was he like when you met him in Alabama? Did he have the long, mantis arms he had when he and I and the rest of us were still living?* John's answer was not audible, because the Dixie Chicks were full tilt on the jukebox, and I am hard of hearing.

We were at Sully's Tavern, a proletarian bar, if ever there was one, where we would always meet, in DeKalb, Illinois, John's corncob town. I would drive an hour and a half there, through the cornfields, from corncob Freeport, Illinois, to meet him, maybe once every couple months, on average, for twenty-some years. And as I was driving, and also on the way back, another hour and a half more, I would wonder to myself, sometimes, why it was always me who drove to meet him, and why he never once came to visit me, except for the two times I invited him to read in Freeport. Was there something wrong with me, was I a loser, an unwelcome guest, a self-pitying depressive, and so forth. Yes, of course I was, but that didn't make me feel any better.

Thus went the story of my life as a minor poet, in the cornfields of northwest Illinois, to be smothered in two-hundred-foot deep ash, three hundred years hence. Oh, I loved Sully's Tavern, in DeKalb, back then, the smell of cheap cologne mixed with spilled beer and menthol cigarettes, and Merle Haggard, Johnny Cash, and Patsy Cline twining the gunmetal air. *What was that you said?* I said, cupping my ear like a frail old man from some mountain holler, against the wailing of the Dixie Chicks.

I said, hollered John, *That No, I don't at all recall him having long "mantis" arms, whatever that means... What a bizarre question to ask. Are you feeling alright?*

One time, long before that, maybe between ten or fifteen thousand years before, while we were still living, I met John Bradley at Bowling Green State University, in Ohio. This was shortly after the two thousand year-old Ezra Pound had died, in Italy, yelling racist oaths in his chair, strapped to the strong stomach of the Vichy-informer Gertrude Stein, who died, herself, at nearly 700 years of age.

We sat next to each other, in a group, with our desks all close together, in the mid-80s, Peter Elbow style, for our professor had arranged us that way, so she could smoke a menthol cigarette and be alone, sitting atop the desk, in a skirt, with her legs casually dangling, in the manner of back then, when teaching English was easy, not that it ever stopped being so after that, until the world ended. I think her name was Barbara. Like all university Poetry professors, she looked to be about four thousand years old.

There was a strong smell of cheap cologne, and I don't know if it came from John, who seemed surly to me on that first meeting (he looked like a Barbary pirate from the 1700s), or if it came from one of the two stylish women in our group, whose names I didn't know and never will, though that is no one's fault, as usual, but mine. I closed my eyes and made believe Hank Williams, in the future, was singing with Mama Carter before the world died forever, as you know it has, if you are here, dreaming that you are reading this review.

His head was transparent, like a vase of crystal from Tirana, where delicate glass was blown for the Iron Curtain trade, into the delicate, beautiful shape of the Great Leader's cochlea, the nautilus of the tympanum. A majestic, ancient oak stood far back inside, far away, down far past the college quad, before it was to be struck by lightning and chopped up to make ladles and clogs, around the time of Srebrenica. Or at least that is what the poem said, as John softly read it, while the pronouns got confused. I could almost see Aimé Césaire, sobbing and sawing it all into proletarian pieces, inside "their" girl-boy head.

Juan (as I would coquettishly come to call him) was nodding all surly at what the ancient students said in fawning reply. And as he did, the limbs of the tree moved to and fro, causing the faces of great, unknown poets from the 15th century Balkans to appear and disappear in its leaves. Yes, I had smoked some hash that James Tate had given me, in Massachusetts, where I was born, in my other dream, long ago, which I had forgotten about for a long time, but now I am remembering. It sure was different!

Also, we were drunk. Suddenly, from across the booth at Sully's, John took my hand and pressed it to his lips and kissed it long, like the Albanian courtier he was, when we were living, which calmed my nerves, those centuries ago. I said to no one in particular, *What are we doing here, three hundred years after we have died?* Three chords sounded from the smoky air and then the whole truth did, too, as in country music. The girls looked at me super strange, for what seemed like a long time.

OK, so the poems veer and swerve and enchant, crack you up and then sadden you, y tanto más… Someone new to Bradley's work, or unaccustomed to reading poetry, might find themselves pleasantly surprised by the absence of all the usual things we expect, and perhaps dread, about contemporary American poesía. These poems, though odd and sometimes downright frightening, are completely clear, comically matter-of-fact, and incredibly easy to read, while also rewarding to releer. Some of the poems end with a real carcajada! On closer reading, the charm of the poems doesn't fade, but a subtle sense of dread, a disintegration of the usual conventions of human behavior and relations, begins to perturbar!

There's something unbottoned and timeless about Bradley's versos. They seem like naughty *fatrasies* written by Philippe de Remi, in 1259, only slightly more esquizofrénico! The narrators of the poem remind me of Twain's personajes. They also have the bumbling, revealing naiveté of Buster Keaton, Charlie Chaplin, and Will Rogers, the innocent American man who keeps discovering he's not so innocent después de todo! That may be, at least partially, the source of these poems' subtle dread: they are, in their own quiet way, an allegory for the self-deluded, so-called normal American vida. (Someone might say the "so-called normal" also includes using, in a review of a white male poet, four white males in a row as illustrative examples of greatness and with no sense of self-awareness, but that's another historia.)

Many of the poems in *Spontaneous Mummification* begin with a simple yet weirdly compelling first line that sets the escena:

"I was born in a box of Cheerios, inside the pantry, near the broom and the bison."

"In Coral Gables, Florida, today, a man invented a new word for *knee*."

"I breathe *allegro calmo senza rigore*, which means my legs rub together calmly yet riotously."

"Jack never makes peepee or poopie, sing Georgette and Rene."

"The President finds a book, *Just and Unjust Wars*, on his Oval Office desk."

"Anne Frank squats over an open book."

In every poem, there is a moment when reality shimmers, and the poem rockets out of something like a tenuous and hyperventilating—but still recognizable—narrative space, to cede its discursive vestments to a wild, waking dream (or pesadilla). Here, hypotactic and syntagmatic norms drop through a neural trapdoor, into a primordial strata of buried parataxis far more elemental than Kantian categories or country music lyrics, y ni decir! Though that said, some of the poems are wrenchingly sad, quite like country, actually; only in this case, the sadness sneaks up on you because of the lack of sentimental manipulation that comes antes! I don't know if I'm making any sense. But just like Matt Zapruder, I am doing my best.

For instance, consider the opening of "For the Black Angel, Oakland Cemetery, Iowa City, Iowa," which I asked John to read me, over the cell, in 1645, when we were once young:

You call yourself Rodina: Rodina Feldevertova: but
I know your name: it's *Before You Worried Away*
Each Thumb: **it's** *When Misshapen Memory Is a Wing*
Rinsed in the Blackened Earth. **I can give you**
a penny: a pen: my sweaty perambulations.

Note for instance, how relaxed the language is, as it stages fantastical propositions in the guise of simple, indexical statements: I both laughed and wept out loud when I read that, feeling something very ancient inside me. In fact, sentí tanta emoción que llamé a mi amigo, el gran poeta y ensayista Andrés Ajens en Santiago, donde reside, y aunque parezca mentira, en una vieja casita situada en pleno terreno que en antaño era parte de las tierras latifundias del padre de Vicente Huidobro. Le dije a mi compa Ajens: Huevón, pues tenés que leer a John Bradley. El hombre es genial!

And then I laughed and wept again as the poem kept on, sending its nine-billion-year-old neutron-star colons into no one's deaf and dumb stun or pain, and far before the little child fell, in Niger, for no reason, down a well:

You look down: away: back to where one day you'll
lead us: to the iron cradle filled with oranges:
still warm from the forge. What was it my father
wanted to tell me: each time in the motel room
when his soft voice: broke: all I could hear was
the rustle of your wings: newspaper singeing
your fingers. I wanted to shake you: shudder
you back into silence: the iron ore before gesture.

Something, you see, that began as gently funny and sweet becomes full
of pathos! And then it is deepened beyond pathos into epistemological
mystery, though not that the latter can't include the former:

You say I fallow the words wrong. I don't know who
I'm saying: what I speak with. One day I'll pause
before a stranger without thumbs: and then whoever
I've stung: however wrong: will I come undone.

I will say, and kill me if it's a lie, that this quatrain stands among the very
greatest of any stanza written in American poetry since the death of César
Vallejo.

Now, the reader should be forewarned that more people die in this book
than in all of Bradley's previous work combined, and more than in any
book by James Tate, I should add. In fact, the living, also, are very dead,
dead as doornails, truth be told. There is a willingness to imagine bodily
decay, disappearance, and the afterlife, without a speck of sentimentality
or self-pity. Mundane actions and objects become symbolic, full of
mysterious resonance! That has always been the strength of Bradley's
work, from his very first book under the spell of James Tate, until his last,
this one, where he transcends him! In that way, the poems are existentially
encouraging. Something interesting is always waiting around an esquina.

Read me another poem, I cried to John, *I just love it when you do, it makes me feel so much better about myself! Even though I know you do not admire me as I do you!* And so he did, in his extinct songbird voice, like sixteen-year old Kasim Omerović of Srebrenica and Emily Dickinson of Amherst, coming together on their virgin wedding bed, eternal and safe in their alabaster chambers.

And then the great Dolly Parton came on the jukebox, sighing a ballad from 16th century Wales. No more or less lost in endless time, really, than the verses of John Bradley. And I could see that almost the whole bar was crying, or trying not to.

John Bradley is the greatest living surrealist poet of the United States of America.

The Following Address Is About Hope

I don't suffer this hurt as César Vallejo. I don't suffer dolor as an artista, as hombre, or even simply as a living being. I don't sufro this dolor as a Catholic, as a Muslim, or as an atheist. Today I only sufro. If mi nombre weren't César Vallejo, I'd sufriría the same dolor. If I weren't an artista, I'd still suffer it. If I weren't hombre, or a living being, even, I'd still suffer it. If I weren't a católico, an ateo, or a mahometano, just the same lo sufriría. Today I sufro from much deeper down. Hoy I just plain sufro.

I hurt now without any explicación. My pain goes so far down that it never had any causa, nor any want of causa. What cause could it have? Where is that thing so exalted that it might cease being its causa? Nada is its cause; nada is able to cease causing it. How has this dolor been birthed as if from itself? Mi dolor es from the north wind and the south wind, like those sexless eggs laid by rare birds fertilized by the viento. If a lover had died, my pain would be completamente the same. If they'd cut my throat to the root, mi dolor sería the same. If life—in short—were otherwise, my pain would be igual. Today I suffer from much further up. Today I sufro solamente.

I gaze upon the hurt of the hungry one, and I see that her hunger is so far from mi sufrimiento that I could keep fasting until muerte-death and at least one blade of grass would always spring from mi tumba-tomb. The same with lovers. How much more thrilled is their sangre-blood compared to mine, which has neither productive source nor use value!

Until now, I'd thought that everything en el universo was inevitably either parent or child. But look: Hoy my dolor is neither parent nor child. It lacks a backbone for twilight, no less than it bears a full breast for dawn, and if they put it in a shuttered room it would not give luz-light; if they put it in a sunlit room it would not cast the slightest shade. Today yo sufro no matter what happens. Hoy simplemente sufro.

(César Abraham Vallejo, translucine by Kent Johnson)